Old and new: a steam and a diesel tug handle the liner 'Caronia' in 1962.

TUGS AND TOWAGE

M. K. Stammers

Shire Publications Ltd

CONTENTS

Printed in Great Britain by C. I. Thomas & Sons (Haverfordwest) Ltd, Press Buildings, Merlins Bridge, Haverfordwest, Dyfed SA61 1XF.

British Library Cataloguing in Publication Data: Stammers, M. K. (Michael K.). Tugs and Towage. 1. Tugs, History. I. Title. 623.8'232'09. ISBN 0-7478-0039-1.

ACKNOWLEDGEMENTS

The author acknowledges with thanks the help given by his wife, colleagues at Merseyside and other maritime museums, preservation organisations and, especially, the assistance of Brian Clarke of Alexandra Towing Company Limited. Illustrations are acknowledged as follows: Alexandra Towing Company Limited, pages 11 (top), 13, 16, 17 (top), 18, 22 (bottom), 23, 24, 30 (bottom); Paul Boot, page 17 (bottom); Bristol Industrial Museum, page 4 (top); Exeter Maritime Museum, page 31; the Maritime Trust, page 27; National Museum and Galleries on Merseyside, pages 1, 19; Southampton Maritime Museum, page 26; Jane Tucker and Nicholas Dean, page 7.

Cover: *A steam tug of the Alexandra Towing Company pulling a Lamport and Holt liner away from the Liverpool Landing Stage about 1930 (from a print of a watercolour by Sam Brown in the Merseyside Maritime Museum collection).*

Below: *Steam tugs helped sailing ships get to sea in adverse winds. These Lowestoft sailing trawlers have been towed out by the tug which can be seen behind the sails. The tug 'Lowestoft' (built at Hull in 1898) is returning to port for more boats.*

Before there were tugs one method of getting in and out of port was to use large oars called sweeps. The crew of this fishing lugger are working their craft at Folkestone in calm weather.

EARLY TUGS

The first tug was the *Charlotte Dundas*. In 1802 this experimental steamboat towed two loaded barges of 70 tons each non-stop along 19½ miles (31 km) of the Forth and Clyde Canal. Although the canal owners feared their banks would be eroded by the wash of steam tugs and the *Charlotte Dundas* was abandoned, steamboats had nevertheless been shown to be a practical means of towing other vessels. Towing with a ship's boats in calm weather and towing canal barges with horses were common practices but steam towage offered far greater power over longer distances than muscles of man or horse. Cargo-carrying sailing ships were often delayed for weeks entering or leaving a port because of unfavourable winds. Ships that had run aground could be towed to safety with the power of steam.

The first steam tugs were all-purpose paddle-steamers. They were used as river and estuary ferries and for towage. Towing ships was more profitable than carrying passengers: timetables were often

disrupted so that a ferry steamer could undertake a towing job. (Hugh Williams, when advertising his new Rock Ferry service across the Mersey in 1822, claimed that his steamers would not be taken off the ferry service for towing.) Steam towage emerged as a separate function on the Tyne and the Clyde by 1830, on the Thames in 1833 and on the Mersey in 1836.

Early tugs were propelled by side-paddles, with low-pressure boilers supplying steam to side-lever engines. These were an adaptation of the well tried, land-based beam engine. They were reliable and simple to maintain. Instead of a large beam on top of the cylinders to transmit the vertical motion of the pistons, they had two beams or side-levers on either side of the cylinders. These lowered the centre of gravity of the engines and improved the tug's stability. After about 1850 many paddle tugs had two of these engines side by side to power each paddle independently. This made

3

Although boiler pressures were low in the first tugs explosions were not unknown and the results were devastating. In November 1866 the Cardiff tug 'Black Eagle No. 1' blew up while towing a barque on the river Avon. The boiler was only three years old.

Paddle tugs were often used as passenger tenders. This Liverpool Steam Tug Company vessel is delivering passengers and their luggage to the ship 'James Baines', bound for the Australian Gold Rush in 1855. Note the skipper standing on the paddle box with the helmsman at the wheel aft.

The power of paddle wheels was improved by 'feathering' equipment. A series of cranks worked by an eccentric altered the angle at which the paddle blades entered the water. Most paddle tugs were fitted with this useful device.

them extremely manoeuvrable, a prime quality in a tug, and enabled steam paddle tugs to remain in service until the 1960s. At first the paddles (floats) were fixed but 'feathering' floats, invented in 1820, altered the angle of the float as it entered the water. This device smoothed the passage of the vessel through the water and saved a large amount of energy.

Experiments with screw-propelled tugs began in 1836. Unlike paddles, the screw propeller was fitted to the stern of the vessel and connected to a steam engine by a shaft. The propeller consisted of a central hub with a number of angled blades (usually three or four) fixed to it. As the screw rotated, with power transmitted from the engine by the shaft, it acted according to the Archimedean screw principle and forced the tug through the water. Because the screw was immersed all the time it produced more power than paddles but did not have their manoeuvring capabilities. There were also technical problems with the building of engines that could turn fast enough to make the screw work efficiently.

The first screw tug, the *Francis B. Ogden*, was built to the design of the Swedish inventor Ericsson. Its trials on the Thames were successful enough to encourage the building of a deep-sea screw-propelled ship, the *Archimedes*, which in turn led to Brunel's revolutionary steamer, the *Great Britain*, in 1843. However, screw propulsion was not adopted for tugs until the 1870s, when efficient high-pressure boilers, compound engines and more effective designs of propeller were available.

Some tug owners preferred to stay with types of vessel that were known to work well. For example, wooden-hulled paddle tugs were still being built on the Tyne (one of the great centres of tug building) until the mid 1880s, long after iron hulls had proved their value.

Nevertheless, from the 1850s tugs grew in size, power and versatility and iron hulls became commonplace. Tug tenders were developed that could both tow large passenger liners and deliver mail, passengers and baggage to them out at anchor.

Tugs went to sea to assist ships in distress, so they had to be built bigger to carry more fuel and to be more seaworthy. One of their regular duties was the towing of rowing lifeboats out of harbour to rescue people from shipwrecks. In the nineteenth century ship-wreck was all too common and many lives were saved through the heroism of both the tug crews and the lifeboatmen. In the Great Gale of 6th January 1839 three American packet-ships outward bound from Liverpool to New York with emigrants went ashore in Liverpool Bay. The tug *Victoria* towed out the lifeboat to the stricken ships but the gale was so bad that the lifeboat herself was forced to run for shelter. The *Victoria* anchored near each wreck and, by slacking off her cable, edged down to pick up some of the passengers. She and another tug returned the next day and rescued another 104 people.

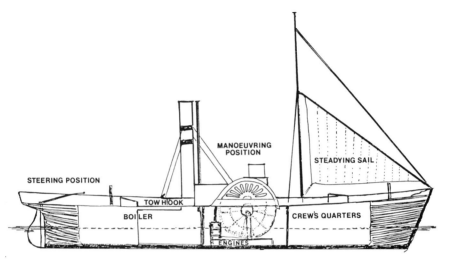

The main features of a paddle tug.

A typical harbour steam tug.

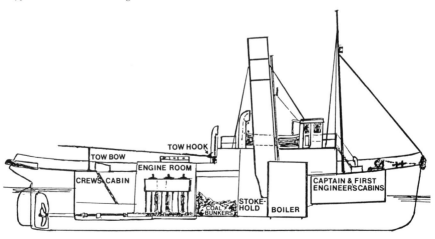

6

Steam towage improved sailing-ship voyage times. American packet-ships like this one could make passages across the Atlantic almost to a timetable.

HARBOUR TUGS

In the late nineteenth century tugs became more specialised. Harbour tugs were and are the most common kind. Their main purpose is to tow large ships in and out of dock, an extremely skilful and sometimes dangerous business. The tug has to manoeuvre large floating objects with little steerage way of their own in confined spaces without damaging other ships and dock installations. Harbour tugs are also used for other undertakings such as firefighting and salvage but these are occasional emergencies, not day-to-day tasks.

When a ship approaches a port her time of arrival can be signalled in advance and tugs can be booked by her agents to meet her off the entrance. In the nineteenth century, before radio, some of the larger harbour tugs would cruise at sea 'seeking' inward-bound vessels. Competition between tug companies, all small-scale businesses, was cut-throat and 'seeking' remained important while the sailing ship was the main ocean carrier. The late nineteenth-century square-rigged ships and four-masted barques of

up to 3000 tons and with small crews had difficulty in confined seas like the English Channel. They often took weeks tacking their way up to the Thames or the Mersey. Towage charges are usually fixed today but sailing-ship masters and tug skippers would frequently bargain on the price of a tow.

An extra attraction of 'seeking' was the chance of encountering a sailing ship running into danger on a lee shore, as a tug that saved a ship in that position could claim salvage. In 1896 the tug *William Jolliffe* was 'seeking' in the Irish Sea: 'next day we were scouring in the vicinity (of Holyhead) for a tow when we sighted a German barque which had suffered damage in the gale. Most of her bulwarks had been carried away and some of her crew had bandaged heads and arms. The vessel had a few sails set and was making good progress. As we came up with her our skipper in an attempt to frighten the master yelled that he was in a very dangerous position but he would take him in tow for a hundred. The old German was not so easily fright-

Above: *Tugs are fitted with a stout fender fixed on the bow, which can be used to push a vessel sideways. Note in the foreground the interesting selection of side fenders on the tug 'Alfred'.*

Left: *Tugs have to manoeuvre large ships through narrow spaces. This calls for great skill and fine judgement on the part of the tug skipper.*

This bow view of the 'Alfred' (1937) in Canning number 2 graving dock, Liverpool (now part of the Merseyside Maritime Museum), shows the typical bow shape of a tug. The deep draught of the hull helped the tug's stability.

ened for he shouted across he would sooner lose her first. Eventually twenty was agreed and we brought the barque to Liverpool.' Outward-bound sailing ships were often towed long distances to get them clear of the land and the danger of shipwreck.

The widespread adoption of screw propellers and of compound steam engines were both important developments. It was important that propellers offered more power because of the increasing size of the steamers being built. Compound engines provided more horsepower and better fuel consumption compared with the traditional side-lever tug engines. The more progressive owners had adopted both these innovations by the 1880s.

The tow-rope is a key component of the tug's equipment. It has to be strong but at the same time elastic to withstand

Ships have to be kept on a short tow-rope in port, as with this Polish sail training ship pictured in the Mersey in 1948.

the many sudden shocks it receives. The minimum size of tow-rope was about 7 inches (173 mm) in circumference. Ropes were made from either manilla, sisal or coir. Man-made fibres are used today, polypropylene or terylene for example, and a length of one of these is usually attached to steel wire rope to give the necessary combination of strength and elasticity. The tow-rope is attached amidships to a towing hook that can swivel, though to keep the tug stable it may be lashed down with a gob rope in a central position while the boat is at work in dock or in sheltered waters. The towing hook has a quick-release mechanism so that the tow can be slipped if the tug is being girded (pulled over) by its charge. An iron frame or frames (the towing bow) on the stern deck keeps the rope away from the deck fittings.

The hull design of a harbour tug is based on a series of compromises. It has to be as short as possible for dock working yet capable of going to sea. It needs a deep draught for stability and to keep the propeller well immersed for maximum power but not so deep that it cannot surmount the sill of the dock gates. The hull must incorporate an engine room, a boiler room (if a steam vessel) and fuel bunkers and also have space for stores, equipment and the crew (average number six men).

The classic form of harbour tug had evolved by 1900. It was about 100 feet (30 metres) long with the steering position well forward (usually without a covering) on a raised deck casing, a tall funnel to provide plenty of draught for the large single Scotch boiler below, a long clear after deck, beneath which were the engines and crew quarters (right over the noisy propeller shaft), and the towing hook located almost amidships for maximum stability. The size of tugs gradually increased and extras (such as a wheelhouse) were added but the basic form was retained. A few owners, for example the Manchester Ship Canal, introduced diesel tugs from the late 1940s but most preferred steam, which was traditional, reliable and easier to maintain. Steam tugs were being launched until the late 1950s, though with oil-fired instead of coal-fired boilers. The Kort nozzle (a steel shroud around the propeller) improved power output and, when a movable version was introduced, manoeuvrability. VHF radio telephones and radar began to be fitted in tugs after the Second World War. The first set on the Mersey, for example, was that installed on the *J. H. Lamey* in 1948.

Above: *A freak accident to the 'South Cock' (1903), aground on a slipway, reveals her Kort nozzle. This metal shroud around her propeller produced more power. Later versions were movable and acted as a rudder.*

Left: *The towing hook was forged steel, usually on a swivel and fitted with a quick release worked from the bridge.*

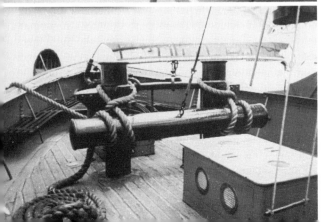

Left: *Heavy bitts were fitted forward and on the side for attaching ropes, for example when the tug was working astern of the tow.*

Tug-tenders were important in ports and anchorages where passenger liners called. They both towed liners and carried passengers, baggage and stores. Many were owned and operated by the liner companies. A typical example was the Cunard Line's 'Skirmisher' (1884), which at 165 feet (50 metres) long and 612 tons gross was much larger than contemporary harbour tugs.

Big ships may need more than one tug. There may be a tug at the bow to steer the ship, together with one at the stern to act as a brake and to stop the stern from swinging while negotiating a narrow entrance. Another tug or tugs may also be needed to push the ship sideways against a quay into its berth. All tugs are fitted with a heavy bow fender for this work. Ships like the Cunard Line's Atlantic express passenger liners required as many as six standard-size harbour tugs.

The revolution in ship design and propulsion since the late 1960s has changed tugs as well as cargo ships.

Deep-sea ships are now much larger, often with higher superstructures or deckloads of containers which catch the wind, and therefore need bigger, more powerful tugs. They are also fitted with bow and possibly stern thrusters (propellers in tunnels across the ship), so that they can often move without tugs. The giant cross-Channel car ferries are a good example.

Today's harbour tug is diesel-engined, producing more than double the brake horsepower and bollard pull of earlier craft. The Alexandra Towing Company's *Collingwood* of 1981 is 107 feet (33

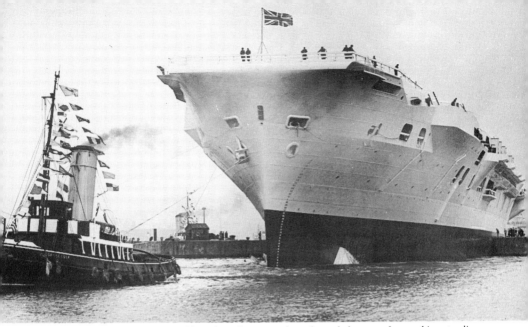

When Britain dominated shipbuilding, launches created much work for tugs. Large ships standing high out of the water, without engines, needed skilful handling. Here, the second 'Ark Royal' is being moved into the fitting-out dock at Cammell Laird's yard at Birkenhead in 1950. The tug 'Grebe Cock' was built in 1935 and broken up in 1967.

metres) overall with 2640 brake horse-power producing 32 tons bollard pull. The same firm's *Collingwood* (formerly *Heath Cock*) of 1958 was 102 feet (31 metres) with one 1060 brake horsepower engine and 15 tons bollard pull.

New propulsion systems have made modern tugs more manoeuvrable, though at the cost of extra mechanical complica-tion. Propellers can have blades whose pitch can be changed according to condi-tions, while patent designs such as the Schottel or Z Peller enable the whole propulsion unit to rotate so that sideways as well as forward and backward thrust can be produced. The popular Voith Schneider system consists of one or two sets of variable-pitch, vertical blades pro-jecting below the hull. Although slightly less powerful than the equivalent screw propeller, they give tugs like the present *Collingwood* superb handling qualities. She, with one of her sisters, is capable of docking container ships of up to 60,000 tons.

The distinction between harbour tugs and seagoing tugs has diminished with the introduction of compact but powerful diesel engines for range and power and better crew quarters built on deck instead of below. The open bridge has long gone and today's tug has what amounts to a 'control tower' with good communica-tions, bridge control of engines and all-round visibility.

The iron steam paddle tug 'Resolute' was the biggest tug of her day (the late 1850s) and heralded a new generation of deep-sea and ocean-going tugs.

At the start of a long-distance tow, the bow tug can be seen with a tow-rope while still in the river. A bridle of anchor chain has been attached on either side of the bow of the tow (the old steam dredger 'Leviathan'); once at sea the bridle was used with a long tow-rope.

After the First World War the cut-throat business of salvage and deep-sea towage became dominated by Dutch towage firms. The only important British company was the United Towing Company of Hull. Here, their tug 'Merchantman' is preparing to tow the Mersey Docks and Harbour Board tender to Spain for scrapping in 1953.

OCEAN-GOING TUGS

Long-distance towing developed from the 'seeking' competition of the harbour tugs. Larger tugs fared better because they were more seaworthy. Salvage provided a powerful incentive. Before the introduction of radio and electronic navigational aids such as radar and echo sounders, strandings were commonplace, especially for sailing ships. Salvage work in the English Channel and around the British Isles led in turn to the recovery of ships damaged in mid ocean.

Long-distance coastal towing was not uncommon in the 1850s. In 1857, for example, the large emigrant ship *Lightning* was chartered to carry troops from London to India to put down the Indian Mutiny. She was towed round from the Mersey to the Thames by the paddle tug *Resolute*, in order to save time. The *Resolute* was then the biggest tug in the world: 161 feet (49.5 metres) long, with 700 indicated horsepower but burning 36

tons of coal a day. This high consumption gave her a range of only 1200 miles (1900 km).

After 1850 British shipyards supplied iron and steel ships to the rest of the world. Deliveries of small coastal and estuary craft and non-propelled vessels such as dredgers or floating docks were either shipped in sections for re-erection at their destination or, more probably, towed out. The bigger tug companies such as Watkins and Elliots of London, the Clyde Shipping Company, Jolliffes, Prendevilles and the Screw Towing Company of Liverpool began to order bigger tugs. In 1875 the Watkins tug *Anglia* was sent to St Helena to tow home the liner *Syria*, which had broken down. This was a record distance of 4300 miles (6900 km). Powerful twin-screw tugs with triple expansion engines extended the towing range still further, combining ocean towing with long-distance coastal work. Sail-

The 'Romsey' was built in 1918 as the Admiralty rescue tug 'Rollcall' to salvage ships damaged in mid ocean by enemy action. At the end of the war she was converted into a tug-tender and excursion vessel. Among her many tasks was attending the launch of the Cunard liner 'Queen Mary' in 1934.

ing ships were often discharged in the Thames or the Mersey and then towed to the Tyne or the South Wales ports in ballast to load an outward cargo of steam coal.

The prime qualities of an ocean-going tug are seaworthiness and range, so that it has to be larger than a harbour or coastal tug. Length is important, as is a raised bow to throw off heavy seas. Deep draught helps stability and keeps the propeller well immersed. Ocean tows, such as broken-down liners or floating docks, catch the wind easily, which makes towing difficult and means that in bad weather the tow can take control. A deep-draught tug can hold her course better than a shallow one. Ocean tugs need to be able to stay at sea for long periods as towing is slow. Range is dictated by fuel capacity and the rate of fuel consumption. Coal-burning tugs had to make use of coaling stations but diesel or diesel-electric engines are more economical and more compact (with no boilers). A system of pumping in water ballast is necessary to maintain draught as fuel is consumed. There must be space

for stores as well as good accommodation for the crew, who have to endure long voyages often in extreme conditions.

In the relatively still water of a harbour a short tow-rope is best but for a deep-sea tow a very long tow-rope is essential. There are many sudden shocks exerted on the rope. The tug may be slowed down climbing a wave while its tow is speeding up, having passed the crest of another. The next moment the conditions could be reversed. The elasticity and length of the rope stop it from snapping: 600 feet (about 200 metres) or more is usual. Tow-ropes parting in mid ocean are not uncommon: it takes great seamanship to reconnect the tow, especially as this kind of accident usually takes place during a gale.

A towing winch helps to even out the shocks on the tow-rope. A wire tow rope is wound on the winch and paid out to the tow. The winch, either hydraulically or electrically driven, can be set to a predetermined load. When this is exceeded the winch will let out more rope and reel it back in when the load has eased. Today harbour tugs often have a winch and most

Towing, mooring and supplying offshore drilling rigs and production platforms has become a major new business for towage companies. The new rig 'Sovereign Explorer' is here being moved from the builder's yard by four large tugs, with the smaller 'Trafalgar' as escort in the foreground.

The preserved tug 'Kerne' started work as a lighterage tug on the Thames and Medway. Originally she had an open bridge; the wheelhouse is a later addition.

The 'Redoubtable' of 1975 was designed for deep-sea work, particularly in the offshore oil business. Note the large stern deck for handling the heavy anchors and chains of oil-drilling rigs.

ocean tugs have a towing hook. If the tug is designed for salvage a large pump will be fitted and there may be other lifting equipment, portable pumps, workshops, diving gear and extra accommodation for a salvage crew.

Submarine attacks in the First World War left many ships immobilised but afloat in mid ocean. The introduction of radio made it possible for them to signal their position. Many commercial tugs were requisitioned for war salvage, supplemented by the rapid building of standard-design rescue tugs. Tugs of the Saint class were 135 feet (45 metres) long and weighed 440 tons, with 1250 indicated horsepower engines. These rescue tugs salvaged 140 ships and assisted five hundred others. They were sold off for commercial service at the end of the war. The *Rollcall*, for example, was converted into a tender tug for the Alexandra Towing Company's new Southampton service.

After 1919 ocean towage and salvage came to be dominated by Dutch firms such as Smit and Company. The old-established British companies such as Jolliffes had either been taken over, were concentrating on harbour work or had gone out of business with the end of regular sailing-ship towing. The only exception was the United Towing Company of Hull, formed in 1921 from a number of small local firms, which expanded its fleet of ocean-going tugs.

Although the diesel engine was introduced for marine use before the First World War and substantially improved in the 1930s, steam engines remained standard for deep-sea tugs, with oil fuel instead of coal.

In the Second World War the Admiralty built large numbers of rescue tugs, most of which were steam-powered, to salvage damaged vessels. Since then, with the improvements in navigational equipment, the amount of salvage work has decreased. However, tugs have played a vital role in many dramatic maritime accidents, for example the unsuccessful attempt to save the listing freighter *Flying Enterprise* and the campaign to control the polluting oil cargo of the wrecked tanker *Torrey Canyon.*

Ships have increased in size and tugs have had to follow. Many of today's harbour tugs are much larger and more powerful than earlier deep-sea tugs and they can operate both inshore and on ocean work.

There is still a need for deep-sea towage of large floating structures. The rise of the offshore oil industry has placed huge demands on tugs. Oil-drilling rigs, pipe-laying barges, floating cranes and production platforms have to be delivered to all parts of the world. Drilling rigs must be precisely positioned, using huge mooring anchors and chains. This calls for an anchor-handling tug, a new kind of ocean-going tug. For instance, Alexandra's *Redoubtable*, built in 1975, is 131 feet (40 metres) long with 5000 brake horsepower diesel engines and a bollard pull of 70 tons. She has a long after deck on which anchors and chains can be stowed.

INLAND WATERWAY TUGS

Towage on canals and rivers (above the highest point that sea-going ships can reach) is chiefly a matter of handling dumb (non-self-propelled) cargo craft: the motor narrow boat tows its dumb 'butty boat'. In some cases the tug itself may also carry cargo. The Weaver steam packets often towed a couple of flats and there were other navigations (like the Aire, the Calder, the Tyne and the Yare) where cargo steamers acted as tugs.

The dimensions of all inland waterway tugs are circumscribed by the size of locks and the depth of water. Fixed bridges (as on the Thames) demand a low superstructure and folding masts and funnels.

Some tugs also have to operate in estuaries and therefore need to carry an anchor, windlass, navigation lights and more than just a day cabin for the crew.

The change from horse to power towing on canals was a slow process that was not completed until the 1950s. Steam tugs such as the first (the *Charlotte Dundas*) and the *Buonaparte* (operating on the Bridgewater Canal in 1803) were tried and rejected because the canal proprietors feared that their speed would wash away the banks. Steam towage was employed extensively by only a few carrying firms, notably Fellows, Morton and Clayton, who in 1876 introduced their

The 'Charlotte Dundas' was the first successful commercial steamer and the first canal tug. Her career was very short because the canal owners feared her wash would erode the canal banks.

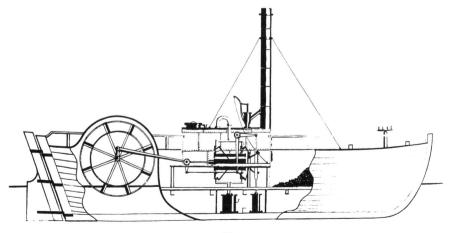

The 'Daniel Adamson' (formerly 'Ralph Brocklebank') was built in 1894. She is laid up at the Boat Museum, Ellesmere Port, but it is intended to restore her to steam. She was designed to tow barges on the Mersey for the Shropshire Union Canal Company. In 1935 she became the directors' boat of the Manchester Ship Canal Company.

own compact type of compound engine for narrow boats.

Simple tugs without a cargo hold were used for special tasks such as towing narrow boats through tunnels. Tugs speeded up the passage through tunnels, which were usually built without a tow-path, and 'legging' a boat through was slow. The earliest, which appears to have been on the Huddersfield Canal, was dragged by means of a cable. Some tunnel tugs were converted to electric power in the twentieth century but the decline in canal traffic and the adoption of diesel engines on narrow boats rapidly made them obsolete.

Towage by tugs that were individual power units was more significant on the larger canals and rivers. They came into their own where it was impossible to build a towpath. Tugs were working on the tidal reaches of the river Trent between Hull and Gainsborough in 1818 and by 1835 on most of the major river estuaries, including the Severn, the Mersey and the Thames. Tugs towed several barges or lighters at once, which brought great savings in transport costs, especially for low-value, bulky commod-ities such as coal or building materials. An inland gasworks (or, later, an electric-ity power station) could receive its coal by water, transhipped from a sea-going

vessel downstream. The tug delivered loaded barges and returned downstream with empty ones.

The Port of London had the most highly developed barging system. Before the building of enclosed docks much of the discharging and loading of sea-going ships had been carried out at river anchorages. Much of the London ware-housing remained upstream even after the building of docks and lighters were a vital part of the inland distribution system of the port. The maximum capacity of a Thames lighter was about 250 tons and so a train of six lighters (the maximum permitted), powered by one small tug, could shift 1500 tons. As recently as 1956 there were 171 steam or motor tugs on the Thames and another eighty launch tugs for working lighters on the upper reaches beyond the Pool. The change to containers and road transport, combined with the shift to Tilbury docks, has reduced Thames lighterage work. Domestic refuse from up-river depots is the major commodity carried today.

Elsewhere, river and canal towage has been abandoned or is carried out on a small scale. British Waterways have small tugs for working barges undertaking bank maintenance and dredging. Some of these are pusher tugs, which are lashed to the stern of a barge or barges (rather like

Above: *Towage of dumb barges or lighters was an essential part of the work of the smaller harbour and inland tugs. The great Port of London could not have existed without their services.*

This river motor tug is towing loaded barges from the Humber up to the mills on the river Hull. Working several loaded barges along a crowded narrow waterway called for as much skill as handling big ships.

The 'Spiller's Rose' is a good representative of the diesel barge tugs that still operate barge traffic. Note the low superstructure and the folding mast to pass under fixed bridges.

attaching an outboard motor to a boat). Pusher tugs, a major feature on the world's great waterways such as the Rhine and the Mississippi, have been successfully operated on the Sheffield and South Yorkshire Navigation, which was improved to carry bigger barges in the 1970s, and on the Thames and Med-way estuaries, particularly in connection with a deep-sea LASH (lighter aboard ship) service. There is probably scope for increasing barge traffic on other major rivers but there seems little likelihood in the near future of a transfer from road transport.

Tug crews worked in all weathers and on all tides. The risks were considerable, especially when working with tow-ropes on the stern deck.

Girding is when the tow takes charge and pulls the tug over. Here, the 'Pea Cock' was getting close to the point of capsize when the tow-rope snapped.

A group of tugs owned by the Liverpool Screw Towing Company, about 1910. This firm, known as 'Cock Tugs' because all their ships had 'Cock' in the name, was one of the pioneers of propeller-driven tugs. Note the lack of superstructure and the open bridges.

TUG OWNERS AND CREWS

Tugs, like all early nineteenth-century steamships, were expensive and risky investments. Until the Limited Liability Act of 1862 the tug owner's personal fortune could be at stake if his tug was wrecked, caused damage or incurred debts. As a result many tugs were owned by groups of people, usually in one port, who subscribed as little as one sixty-fourth (a traditional share) of the total sum raised for purchasing a tug. The shareholders, who might be business associates, friends or relatives, normally placed the day-to-day management of the tug in the hands of a manager, who would receive a percentage of the earnings (before a dividend was declared) for his work.

The first recognised tug owners were William Watkins and Company who in 1833 established their towage business on the Thames with the paddle tug *Monarch*. (This tug was immortalised by Turner in his painting of the wooden warship *Téméraire*.)

All the early companies were based on particular estuaries or ports but there was often fierce local competition, notably on the Tyne, because of the large number of single tug owners. When Watkins tried to invade the Mersey in 1853 they were successfully resisted by the half dozen local fleets. Competition for harbour and sea towage remained intense throughout the nineteenth century: companies were established and wound up regularly. There were plenty of opportunities for the enterprising owner. For example, around 1880 a group of Thames river pilots formed their own towage business, the Gamecock Steam Towing Company, which was able to compete against well established firms such as William Watkins.

Most tug owners specialised in towage. Although they might have barge tugs and ship-handling tugs, they tended not to embark on other kinds of ship-owning. There were important exceptions: the Clyde Shipping Company owned deep-sea and coastal cargo ships and many of the big passenger lines, such as White

Tug skippers usually started their careers as deckhands: experience was needed rather than theoretical knowledge. These skippers are in charge of the launch of the aircraft carrier 'Ark Royal' in 1950.

Star, Canadian Pacific and Cunard, maintained tug-tenders to assist their ships. Many statutory authorities, such as the Port of London Authority, the Manchester Ship Canal and various harbour boards, owned their own tugs for ship handling and dock maintenance work.

From the beginning of the twentieth century there was a tendency for tug firms, which were largely family affairs, to merge into larger units and for the larger firms to move into ports outside their main base. The Alexandra Towing Company, for example, took over the important firm of Jolliffes in 1908 and expanded to Swansea and Southampton in the 1920s. Elliots, Watkins and Gamecock tugs on the Thames formed Ship Towage (London) in 1950. In 1969 they added Sun Tugs and in 1975 they were taken over by Alexandra Towing, originally of Liverpool but now with a nationwide service.

The average harbour tug carried five or six men: master, mate, engineer, fireman and two deckhands. Canal and other small tugs might have just two crew,

while an ocean-going salvage tug could accommodate a large crew plus specialists such as divers and surveyors. Most tugs today, in spite of their increased size and power, still carry six men. Diesel engines, automated controls and winches for rope handling make this possible.

The crew was recruited from the tug's home port. In contrast to many deep-sea ships, tug crews tended to stay on the same ship or with the same company. Sons followed fathers into the tugs. A young man might start work as either a deckhand or a fireman. As a deckhand he helped the mate with handling the ropes and the maintenance of the vessel, ran errands for the skipper and learned how to steer the ship and handle the engine-room controls. There was no formal training. Eventually, when a vacancy arose, he might be promoted to mate and ultimately to master. The same procedure applied to the firemen.

Tug handling demanded great skill learned through experience. In steam tugs it also called for teamwork. Unlike today, there were no automated engine

24

Tugs were built in many small shipyards. Today, with the decline of shipbuilding in the United Kingdom, only a handful survive. This is the launching ceremony for the diesel tug 'Egerton' at Yarwood's shipyard, Northwich, Cheshire, on 17th December 1964.

Many tugs went through several changes of ownership. This tug was built in 1903 for the Clyde Shipping Company as 'Flying Swift' but became successively 'Torbay Scout', 'Heathercock' (as in the picture) and 'Loyal Briton' before being scrapped in 1957.

rooms: orders were relayed to the engineer by the engine-room telegraph and a voice pipe. Through experience the engineer could anticipate the master's requirements and ensure that the engines would respond quickly. The fireman had to keep up steam pressure in the boiler, which meant not simply shovelling on more coal but also skilfully raking out all the ashes and clinker without letting the pressure drop. Everyone had to work flexibly: the mate and deckhands helped the engine-room crew to put coal in the bunkers and tip the ashes over the side and the engineers helped with deck jobs that needed extra manpower.

The hours were long and arduous. Steam had to be raised. There was no question of an instant start as with a diesel engine. The tug had to be available at any time of the day or night, according to the times of the tides. This often led to long hours of waiting and, for a 'seeking' tug, several days at sea. The rope-handling work on deck was heavy and dangerous. Sometimes a tow-rope broke under strain and whiplashed across the deck causing severe injury to anyone in the way. Tugs were sometimes girded by their tows and the crews drowned. Before the benefit of radar there were collisions with larger ships and the tug usually came off worse. Tug-boat accommodation was not of the highest standard, with a crew cabin aft over the propeller and separate cabins for the master and engineer forward under the bridge.

Whatever the hardships, there were some compensations. There was a freedom and comradeship working on a tug which was not always found on bigger ships. The crew did not have to endure the isolation and absence from family of a long ocean voyage. There was also the possibility of command and even, in some cases, of ownership of a tug. Many of the nineteenth-century Tyne tugs were skipper-owned. Elsewhere, there were examples of men such as Edward Nicholson of Great Yarmouth, who started as a fireman and eventually became the owner-manager of a fleet of four tugs.

The tug-tender 'Calshot' is the sole survivor of this type of tug. As this photograph shows, she was built as a steamer and was converted to diesel in the 1960s. Southampton Maritime Museum has acquired this ship, which was built and based at Southampton.

The award-winning 'Portwey' belongs to the Maritime Trust and is run by a highly professional group of volunteers. She worked on the Dart and is today based at West India Dock, London.

TUGS TODAY

Tugs are not as numerous as they were but they have become bigger, more powerful and more versatile. There are fewer deep-sea ships and much less barge traffic. The old companies have gradually merged into larger units working several ports. (The Alexandra Towing Company is the biggest British firm with over fifty tugs based at Liverpool, Swansea, Southampton, London, the Medway, Felixstowe, Gibraltar and Port Pleasant in the Falkland Islands.) The number of tug builders has also diminished. The traditional tug-building centre, the Tyne, has long gone and there are half a dozen scattered yards, on the Humber, in Lowestoft, on the Mersey and elsewhere, building new vessels. As with deep-sea ships, only a few British-built tugs have been constructed for overseas customers in the 1980s.

Tugs usually have a very long working life in comparison to cargo and passenger ships. Many steam tugs worked for over fifty years, after which their hulls were still in good enough condition to be converted to diesel engines. The oldest tug now working commercially is the *Primrose*, belonging to the Laxey Towing Company, Isle of Man, and built in 1890. Many British steam tugs built in the 1950s were sold abroad, especially to Greece and Italy, where they were in service for over thirty years.

Steam tugs have attracted the attention of steam preservationists and maritime museums: they are small in size and so suitable for a volunteer group or small museum to maintain. Tugs are good subjects for preservation because, despite their size, they exhibit most of the features of larger ships. It would be virtually impossible to preserve a coaster of 1000 tons for any length of time, but a tug (apart from the cargo space) has similar features on the bridge, in the engine room and in the crew accommodation.

Most tugs are kept statically afloat but often retain the capability of raising steam. Bristol Industrial Museum has restored its Sharpness Canal tug *May* to working condition, making her the oldest

27

Canal tug 'Enterprise No. 1' (now restored) could pull up to nine 'Joey' boats carrying 100 tons on the canals of the Black Country.

Many narrow canal boats were worked in pairs with a powered boat towing a 'dumb' or 'butty' boat. The 'President', owned by the Black Country Museum, is the only working example of a steam-powered narrow boat.

working tug. Steam has more romance than diesel but the Boat Museum (in Ellesmere Port, Cheshire) has preserved the tug *Worcester* with its early Bolinder diesel engine.

Tug preservation, like any other kind of ship preservation, is very expensive, especially when the vessel is kept in operating condition. There are strict regulations on safety, structural integrity and operating procedures laid down by the Department of Trade and Industry and insurance companies. Tugs are, however, built with great strength. The *Kerne* of 1913 has plating that is half an inch (13 mm) thick. Simple and robust compound or triple expansion engines are durable and individual components can be removed and replaced easily. Boilers and fireboxes, if large structures, are also relatively simple. Provided the outer shell is in good condition a boiler can be maintained with regular replacements of the internal parts, such as tubes and firebars, that suffer from extreme heat. The ship also has to be regularly docked and painted. Coal is very expensive and several tons can be consumed in a weekend.

It is therefore not surprising that it is smaller river and harbour tugs that are kept in steam. Several much larger vessels are the subject of preservation projects but are afloat with their engines and boilers 'mothballed'. The fine sea-going *St Canute* at Exeter Maritime Museum is one example. She can be visited by the public, who can see every part of the ship from the bridge to the engine room: only the steam and the heat are missing.

The ultimate form of ship preservation is to take the vessel out of the hostile water environment. At the National Maritime Museum the paddle tug *Reliant* was cut into sections and rebuilt in the Neptune Hall. This was very expensive to carry out but the effect is striking, especially when her side-lever engine and paddle are turned by an electric motor. Her sister tug, the *Eppleton Hall*, was steamed out to San Francisco but is deteriorating and it is likely that the *Reliant* will be the only paddle tug to survive.

Most classes of tug are represented in the preservation fleet. Southampton has

The TID class of tugs was introduced in 1943 for lighterage and dock work. They were designed for simple speedy building, with straight rather than curved plates in the hull. Over 180 such craft were built. TID 184, built in 1945, worked in Rosyth naval dockyard until 1974. She is now kept in steaming condition by the Medway Maritime Museum.

a passenger tender-tug; the Manchester Ship Canal directors' boat *Daniel Adamson* at the Boat Museum fulfilled a similar purpose. Canal tugs and harbour tugs are well covered but there is as yet no ocean-going salvage or anchor-handling tug on display in the United Kingdom. However, in the German National Maritime Museum in Bremerhaven there is a superb salvage tug, the *Seefalke* of 1924, as well as the first working Voith Schneider tug, the *Stier* of 1954.

Tugs are attractive and distinctive ships with a vital function and are unlikely to be replaced in the foreseeable future.

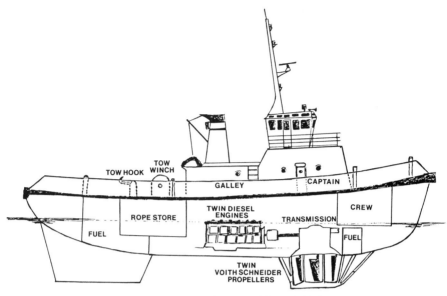

The Voith Schneider propulsion system depends on variable-pitch blades projecting below the hull, protected by a cage. The tug is steered as well as powered by these blades; no rudder is needed.

All deep-sea ships need a tug's aid in port, including the royal yacht 'Britannia'. The 'North Light' is here pulling her away from the Liverpool Landing Stage in 1957.

The 'St Canute' is the largest exhibit of the Exeter Maritime Museum. Built in Denmark in 1931, she is a fine example of a deep-sea tug. She worked at Fowey from 1958 to 1969 and was then adopted by the museum for preservation.

FURTHER READING

BOOKS
Bowen, F. C. *100 Years of Towage*. Watkins, 1933.
Hallam, B. *Blow Five*. Journal of Commerce, 1976.
McMurray, H. C. *Old Order, New Thing*. HMSO, 1972.
Thomas, P. N. *British Steam Tugs*. Waine Research, 1983.
Weaver, C. P. and C. R. *Steam on Canals*. David and Charles, 1981.

PERIODICALS
Sea Breezes (monthly): 202 Cotton Exchange Building, Old Hall Street, Liverpool L3 9LA.
Ships Monthly: Kottingham House, Dale Street, Burton upon Trent, Staffordshire DE14 3TD.
Ship and Boat International (ten issues a year): 3 Park Terrace, Worcester Park, Surrey.

PLACES TO VISIT

Britain's maritime museums contain a wealth of preserved craft, models, archives and pictures that will repay study by anyone interested in tugs and towage. Intending visitors are advised to check times of opening before making a special journey. Sites marked with an asterisk have historic tugs that can be seen only from the quayside and there is no public access on board.

The Boat Museum, Dockyard Road, Ellesmere Port, Cheshire L65 4EF. Telephone: 051-355 5017. Manchester Ship Canal tender *Daniel Adamson* (1903), canal tunnel tug *Worcester* (1908-12), several small canal tugs including *Birchills* (1912), *Aleida* (1939) and *Beeston* (1946). Also, occasionally, the steam tug *Kerne* (1913), at present under repair at Birkenhead.*

Bristol Industrial Museum, Prince's Wharf, Prince Street, Bristol, Avon BS1 4RN. Telephone: 0272 299771 extension 290. The steam tug *May* (1861), the oldest working tug.*

East Kent Maritime Museum, Clock House, Pier Yard, Royal Harbour, Ramsgate, Kent CT11 8LS. Telephone: 0843 587765. Steam tug *Cervia* (1946).*

Exeter Maritime Museum, The Haven, Exeter, Devon EX2 8DT. Telephone: 0392 58075. Steam tug *St Canute* (1931).

Falmouth Maritime Museum, 2 Bell's Court, off Market Street, Falmouth, Cornwall. Telephone: 0326 318107 or 250507. Steam tug *St Denys* (1929) at Custom House Quay, Falmouth.

Maldon. Privately owned steam tug *Brent* (1945) is based on Maldon, Essex, but not there permanently as she is in steaming condition.

Maryport Maritime Museum, 1 Senhouse Street, Shipping Brow, Maryport, Cumbria CA15 6AB. Telephone: 090081 3738. Though not directly associated with the museum, the steam tugs *Chipchase* (1953) and *Harecraig II* (1951) are preserved in the nearby docks.*

Medway Maritime Museum, c/o Chatham Historic Dockyard, Chatham, Kent. Steam paddle tug *John H. Amos* (1931) and tug *TID 64*.*

Merseyside Maritime Museum, Albert Dock, Liverpool, Merseyside L3 4AA. Telephone: 051-709 1551. Steam tug *Kerne* (1913) is based here occasionally.*

National Maritime Museum, Romney Road, Greenwich, London SE10 9NF. Telephone: 01-858 4422. Steam paddle tug *Reliant* (1907) built into the Neptune Hall exhibitions.

National Waterways Museum, Llanthony Warehouse, Gloucester Docks, Gloucester GL1 2EH. Telephone: 0452 25524. Displays include a sectioned full-size Bantam tug of about 1946-7.

St Katharine's Dock, London E1 9LB. Steam tug *Challenge*.*

Scottish Maritime Museum, Laird Forge, Gottries Road, Irvine, Ayrshire KA12 3QE. Telephone: 0294 78283. Motor tug *Garnock* (1956).

Swansea Maritime and Industrial Museum, Museum Square, Maritime Quarter, Swansea, West Glamorgan SA1 1SN. Telephone: 0792 50351. Steam tug *Canning* (1954).

Welsh Industrial and Maritime Museum, Bute Street, Cardiff, South Glamorgan. Telephone: 0222 481919. Steam tug *Sea Alarm* (1941).

West India Dock, Poplar, London E14. Maritime Trust tug *Portwey* and the London Museum's *Knocker White* laid up here.* *Portwey* is kept steaming by the Friends of Portwey, c/o 72 Downs Road, Coulsdon, Surrey CR3 1AF.